UP CLOSE

REPTILES & AMPHIBIANS

A CLOSE-UP PHOTOGRAPHIC LOOK INSIDE YOUR WORLD

Written by Heidi Fiedler

Quarto is the authority on a wide range of topics.
Quarto educates, entertains, and enriches the lives of our readers—
enthusiasts and lovers of hands-on living.
www.quartoknows.com

© 2016 Quarto Publishing Group USA Inc.
Published by Walter Foster Jr., an imprint of Quarto Publishing Group USA Inc.
All rights reserved. Walter Foster Jr. is trademarked.

Project Editor: Heidi Fiedler
Written by Heidi Fiedler

Photographs on pages 41, 42, and 50 by Igor Siwanowicz. Photograph on page 38 by John Crux.
Photograph on pages 14–15 by Danté Fenolio / Science Source.
Photographs on page 20 and 60 by Steve Gschmeissner / Science Source.
Cover photography and all other images © Shutterstock.

6 Orchard Road, Suite 100
Lake Forest, CA 92630
quartoknows.com
Visit our blogs @quartoknows.com

MIX
Paper from
responsible sources
FSC® C017606

Printed in China
1 3 5 7 9 10 8 6 4 2

Are You Ready for Your Close-up?

Look!
Closer…
Closer…
Closer…
Can you feel your brain tickling? That's the magic of looking at something way UP CLOSE. It can transform the ordinary into something new and strange and inspires everyone from hi-tech shutterbugs to supersmart scientists to look again. So let's turn the ZOOM up to eleven and discover a whole new way of seeing the world.

How Eye See the World

"Whatcha lookin' at?" That's the question people have been asking each other for thousands of years. The first humans observed interesting—and important—things like woolly mammoths, lightning, and each other. Early artists moved on to painting and drawing what they saw. Finally, in 1862, photography allowed people to capture what they saw in new and amazing ways.

Today, photographs are everywhere. Cereal boxes, bulletin boards, and T-shirts are all home to photos. A simple image search online can produce adorable images of bright-eyed babies or stark, white, snowy landscapes. Photographers capture everything from moments of joy and pain to the wonders that exist in the cracks and hidden layers of our busy world. They focus their attention on a huge range of subjects, and the images they produce reveal how everyone sees the world in their own unique way.

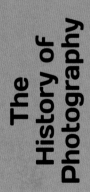

The History of Photography

| Black & White Photography | **1839** Daguerreotypes capture rough images. | **1859** Photography goes panoramic. | **1862** Nicéphore Niépce creates the first photograph. It takes 8 hours. | **1877** Eadweard Muybridge invents a way to shoot objects—like horses—in motion. |

Color Photography

1888
Kodak™ produces the first mass-produced camera.

1912
The 35mm camera takes center stage.

1930
Flash bulbs help photographers capture images in low light.

1935
New techniques make color photography shine.

1939
An electron microscope reveals what a virus looks like.

1946
Zoomar produces the zoom lens.

Digital Photography

1976
Canon® produces the first camera with a microprocessor.

"**Photography**...has **little** to do with the things you **see** and **everything** to do with the **way** you **see** them."
—Elliott Erwitt

1992
The first JPEG is produced.

2015
Instagram is home to over 20 billion images.

Extreme Close-up!

Photography has been helping people express how they see the world for nearly 200 years, and in that time, things have gone way beyond taking a simple shot of a horse or a sunset. Today, photographers are pushing the limits of technology.

Macro photographers use large lenses to get WAY up close to their subjects. They can magnify an object up to five times its size, with special lenses that reveal patterns and textures that wow viewers.

Micro photography goes even further. It uses a microscope to reveal details humans could never see before. It can make a blood cell look like a glowing planet or a priceless jewel.

With their vibrant colors and strange bodies, reptiles and amphibians are a favorite subject for photographers. Some shutterbugs are scientists studying the surface of a lizard's tongue in intense detail. Others are enthusiasts obsessed with capturing every scale on a snake. Together, their images help us see the natural world in a whole new way. Take a look!

Getting the Shot

Photographers choose where and how they want to work based on what type of images they want to produce.

Out in the Field
Macro photographers can take their giant lenses outside to capture animals in their natural environment.

In the Studio
Working inside lets photographers have more control over the lighting, the angle of the camera, and their subjects.

Under the Microscope
A microscope allows photographers to look at anatomy, such as a cluster of blood cells, in even more detail.

Colorful Language

Deep thinkers as far back as Aristotle have admired the chameleon's ability to change colors. Today scientists believe green and yellow streaks mean, "I'm relaxed." Orange and red seem to say, "I'm ready to mate" or "I'm stressed." In a fight, brown means, "You win. I give up." Chameleons with brighter colors tend to start more fights. But watch out! It's usually the chameleons that change colors more quickly that win.

Gotcha!

A chameleon's powerful tongue works a bit like a bow and arrow, but one that brings back insects. In cold weather, other muscles may slow, but not the tongue muscles. They're always ready to spring into action and grab a bite to eat.

Scientific Name:
    Furcifer pardalis
Size: 10 to 20 inches
Habitat: Forests of Madagascar and other parts of Africa
Diet: Insects and worms

Breeders arrange **chameleon** cages so **females** can't see males, and **males** can't see any other chameleons. If they see each other, they'll try to attack.

Sweet Cheeks

Most amphibians begin life as eggs, grow into larvae that live underwater, and then take on a new adult form that can survive on land. But axolotls never really grow out of that super cute, pinch-your-cheeks stage. Full-grown axolotl salamanders have lungs, but still rely on the gills that grow from their heads to survive. And they need as much protection as a baby: These strange-but-true creatures are on the endangered species list.

A Superpowered Salamander

Many amphibians can regrow arms and legs, but axolotls can also regrow jaws, spines, and even their brains! Scientists are studying these salamanders to learn how humans might one day be able to do the same.

Scientific Name:
   Ambystoma mexicanum
Size: Up to 12 inches
Habitat: Lakes near Mexico City
Diet: Mollusks, worms, insects, and small fish

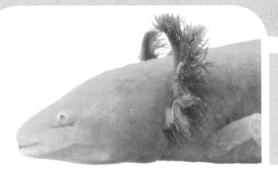

Axolotls come in nearly every color of the **rainbow**, and many are albino.

Hunting for Cover

High in the branches of the Australian tropics, green tree pythons watch for prey. When they spot a tasty meal, they dangle like long vines to attract attention or launch a sneak attack. Despite their name, green tree pythons aren't born green. Hatchlings are yellow or red, so they blend in with patches of light on the rain forest floor, where they first live. When the pythons are big enough to hunt the larger prey that lives in the treetops, they turn green.

Mutants and Morphs

Reptile breeders are developing morphs, versions of a species that are rarely found in the wild. They mate the species that will produce interesting mutations, including pythons of all different colors.

Scientific Name: Morelia viridis
Size: 4 to 6 feet
Habitat: Tropics of Australia and nearby islands
Diet: Small reptiles, invertebrates, mammals, and birds

Pythons use the pits around their mouths to detect **heat** and find prey at night.

Underwater, tiny tadpoles transform into...

Ghosts of the Rain Forest

Every frog starts its life as a tadpole with a tail and gills. But not every tadpole turns into a frog that has an underbelly as clear as glass. Seen from above, these glass frogs blend in with the leaves they like to sit on. But from below, major veins, leg bones, the gall bladder, intestines, and a bright red heart can all be seen pulsing with life.

Scientific Name:
    Hyalinobatrachium iaspidiense
Size: 1 inch
Habitat: Trees of Central and South American rain forests
Diet: Small insects

Chirrrp! Peep! Trill!
Forget croaking, this frog **whistles** like an insect.

Looking Ahead
Most frogs have eyes on the sides of their heads, so they can watch for predators that might be approaching. Glass frogs have eyes that face forward, so they can easily find prey in front of them. Once they have a target in sight, they leap with their mouths wide open and gulp down whatever they catch.

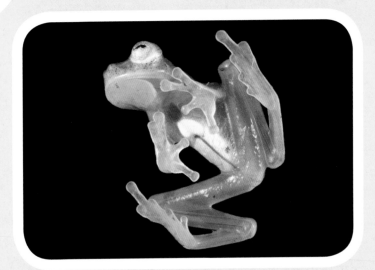

Standing Tall

Most reptiles don't make a lot of noise, but when it comes to telling each other who's boss, their body language is loud and clear. Iguanas defend their territory and attract mates with push-ups, head bobs, and flared dewlaps. But iguana standoffs aren't always so subtle. When it's time for battle, they leap into action and snap their long tails like powerful whips.

Scientific Name:
Iguana iguana
Size: 5 to 7 feet
Habitat: Trees of Central and South America
Diet: Leaves, flowers, fruit, and insects

No Humans Allowed

Ever want to live in a tree house and never come down? Iguanas spend most of their time doing just that. They visit the ground only to mate, lay eggs, or move to a different tree.

Iguanas have special **muscles** that allow them to **detach** their **tails** and grow another when they need to distract predators.

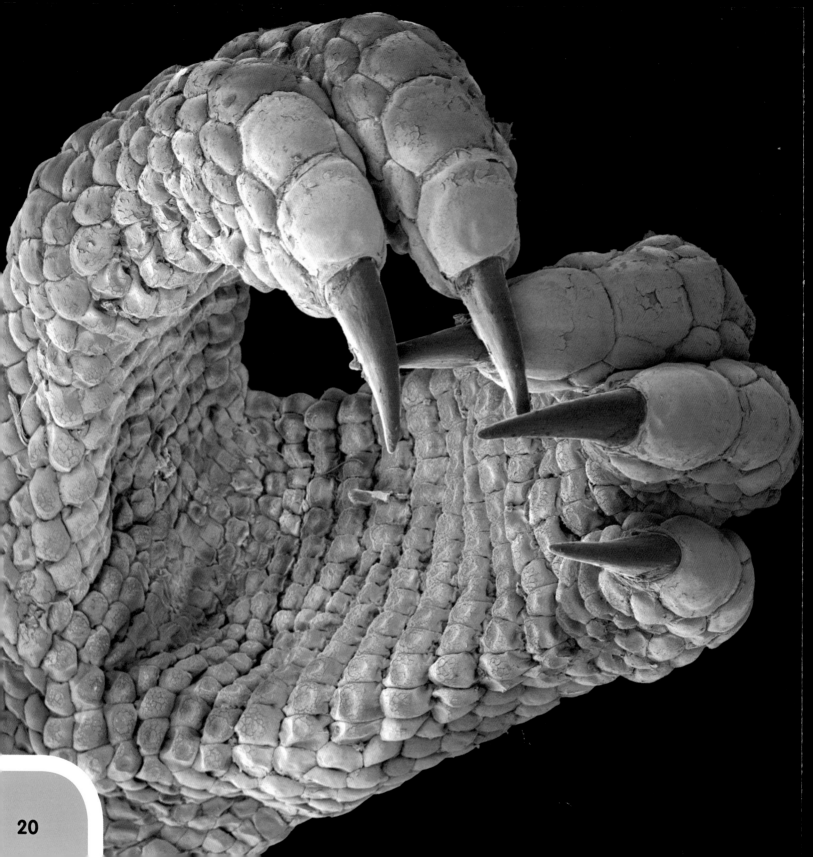

Sharper than Stilettos

Chameleons are famous for their fabulous colors. But with two toes pointing forward and two toes back, it's scandalous to ignore their fiercely fashionable feet. Chameleons are the only lizards that can pinch their toes together like a hand. This helps them grip branches and makes them ultra-strong climbers.

Sharp claws help **chameleons** steady themselves as they **scale** trees.

Beyond X-Ray Vision

Scientists use scanning electron microscopes (SEMs) to get way up close to their subjects. Subjects are often stained or dipped in metal. To create an image, the SEM hits the subject with electrons and records how it bounces back.

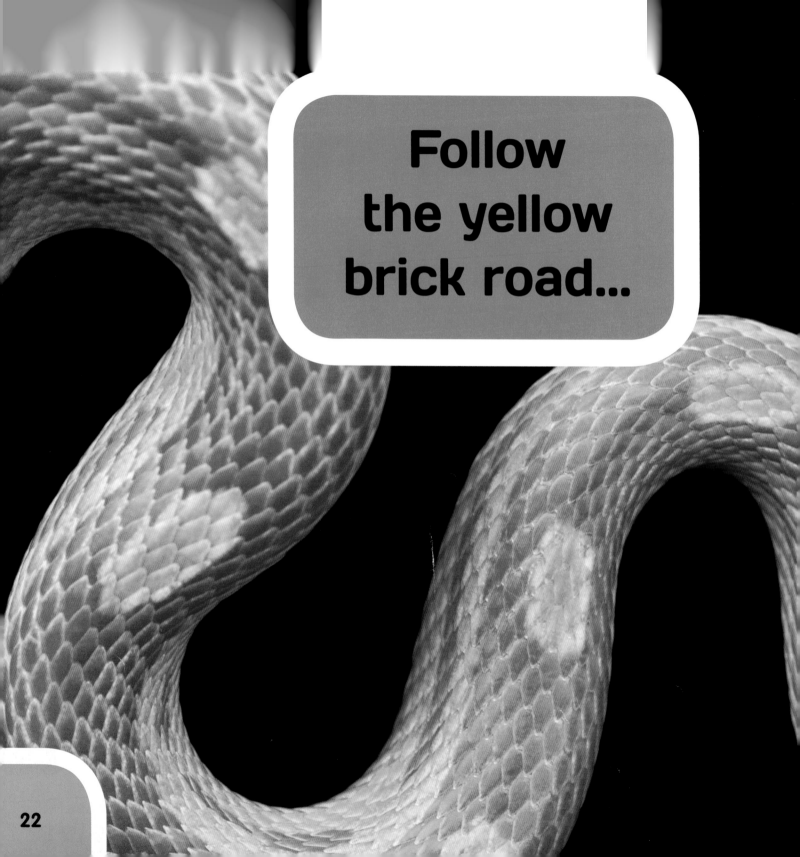

Follow
the yellow
brick road...

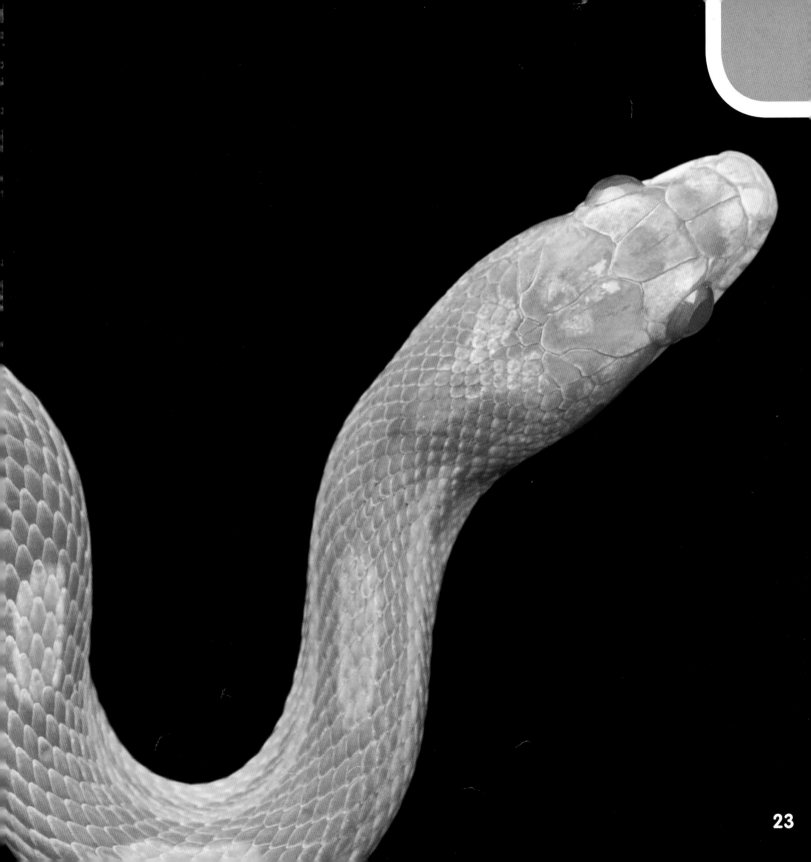

To Snake Road

Why did the corn snake cross the road? To slither to dry land! Every year, thousands of snakes and other reptiles travel from the limestone bluffs in Shawnee National Forest to the wetlands of LaRue Swamp. In the fall, they return to the forest to hibernate in the rocks where it's dry. During migration season, the trail is closed to cars, but humans are welcome to walk across Snake Road—if they dare.

Slithering Near and Far

Snakes also gather to form massive mating balls. In Manitoba, Canada, 75,000 red-sided garter snakes slide into a pit to mate every spring. Males try to attract attention by rubbing the heads of females. The snakes return to the same den each year.

Snakes are found on every continent except **Antarctica.**

Scientific Name: Pantherophis guttatus
Size: 2 to 6 feet
Habitat: Meadows in the United States
Diet: Lizards, frogs, mice, birds, and bats

Zen Master

Imagine spending your days sitting perfectly still, watching the world go by. Waiting. Watching. Waiting. Jump! Devour a cricket, and return to your rock. Waiting. Watching. Waiting. Watching… The Vietnamese mossy frog is the master of waiting and watching. How does it stay so zen? It probably helps knowing it's hidden from view. This strange frog has developed warts and spines that help it blend in to the moss that grows in the flooded caves where it lives…just watching the world go by.

When they're scared, **mossy frogs** curl into a ball and play dead like a **roly poly**!

Scientific Name:
Theloderma corticale
Size: Up to 3.5 inches
Habitat: Mountains of Vietnam
Diet: Small insects

Frog or Toad?

All toads are frogs, but not all frogs are toads. They're both amphibians, which means they live in water and on land. But frogs usually spend most of their time in water, and toads prefer to live on land. Most frogs have smooth, moist skin, while toads have dry, pebbly skin. Frogs are also thinner and have longer legs than toads.

frog

toad

The Bearded Lady

Meeting a bearded dragon? Don't assume it's male. Both males and females have spiky dewlap beards. When they're on high alert, their beards grow. If things get really aggressive, they turn black. And you better believe there's going to be some head bobbing. Still want to make friends with a bearded dragon? Try slowly waving your arm in a circle. That's how beardies show each other they're both bearded dragons.

The color of a **beardie** depends on the **color** of the **soil** where it lives.

Scientific Name:
  Pogona vitticeps
Size: 1 to 2 feet
Habitat: Australia
Diet: Plants, insects,
  small rodents, and
  lizards

Nap Time

When bearded dragons can't find enough food or the weather is harsh, they hide out underground and take a long nap. If needed, they can stay dormant for weeks. When cold-blooded animals enter this state, it's called "brumation," which sounds like rumination, but involves a lot less thinking.

Fangs straight
from the Triassic?

The truth
is even scarier...

Survival of the Fiercest

There were once as many different types of crocodiles as there were dinosaurs. Some early crocodile ancestors had stubby tales. Others had smooth skin and large fins like dolphins. Some were even herbivores. The crocodiles that survived were terrifying killers. Over time, they've devoured everything from prehistoric lizards to modern mammals. The crocodiles with the deadliest teeth evolved to become the modern monsters that roam the Earth today.

Croc or Gator?

If an alligator has its mouth closed, you might not see many teeth, but on a crocodile, there will be plenty of big chompers visible. Alligators have wider snouts, while crocodiles' mouths are pointier. Gators also have darker, greener skin. Alligators tend to live in freshwater, while most crocodiles prefer saltwater.

Scientific Name: Crocodylus porosus
Size: Up to 23 feet
Habitat: Australia and Asia
Diet: Buffalo, boar, monkeys, turtles, snakes, and birds

The nostrils on **Purussaurus**, an early relative of the **crocodile**, were larger than a **human head!**

Keeping Watch

In the animal kingdom, eyes come in a wide variety of styles. Nocturnal animals tend to have slits for pupils, while animals that are active in the day have round pupils. Many lizards have a third eye that acts like a compass, allowing them to steer by the sun.

Eyelids are optional. Amphibians and most lizards have them, but snakes don't, although they do shed a clear piece of skin from their eyes when they molt. Whatever their shape, all eyes help reptiles and amphibians hunt for prey and watch for predators.

Blue Eye-guana

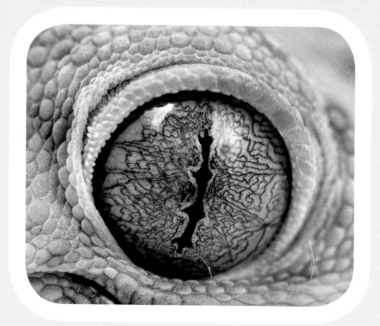

Wormhole to Planet Gecko

Raising an Eyebrow

Dangerous Dilation

Serious Red Eye

Caiman Close Up

A Real Mouthful

These green guys are sometimes called Pac-Man frogs, and they have the appetite to match. Amazon horned frogs swallow their prey whole and then dig in with their sharp teeth. They'll eat pretty much anything that's smaller than them—and sometimes animals that aren't! These frogs have eyes bigger than their stomachs *and* their mouths. Some hungry frogs have been found dead with victims that were too big to swallow still hanging from their jaws.

Scientific Name:
   Ceratophrys cornuta
Size: 4 to 6 inches
Habitat: Near freshwater
   pools in South America
Diet: Any animal it can get
   its mouth around

Meanwhile, in **Australia**, the **gastric brooding frog** gives birth through its mouth!

A Deadly Disguise

Horned frogs surprise prey by hiding on the forest floor. Their horns blend in with the leaves on the ground, where they can quietly wait for the right moment to strike.

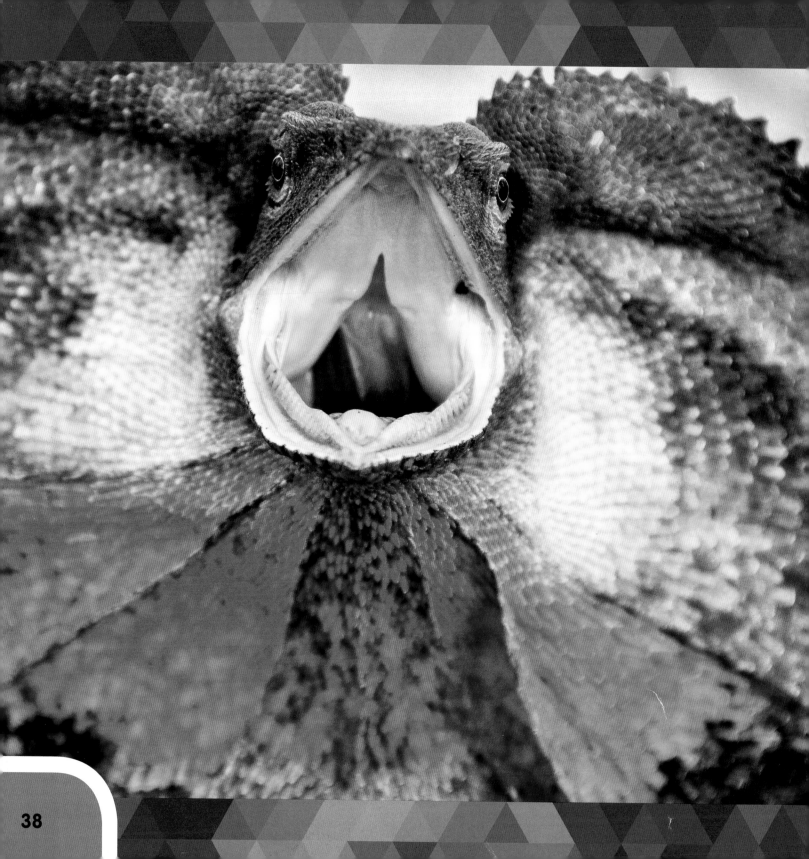

Heads Will Roll!

When a frilled-neck feels threatened, it unfurls a ruff as grand as any worn by an Elizabethan king. Frills can reach up to 12 inches across, which makes their owners look royally scary to predators. When threatened, this lizard orders predators to retreat with a hiss. If that doesn't work, it will lash out with its tail, take a bite, or run back to its tree throne.

Scientific Name:
    Chlamydosaurus kingii
Size: 3 feet
Habitat: Northern
    Australia
Diet: Insects, small lizards, and small mammals

The **frilled-neck lizard** is also known as the "frilled dragon." A **mini** dragon, but still a dragon!

Catch Me If You Can

Try chasing a frilled lizard, and you'll find it can run surprisingly fast. When it's time to hit the road, it rises up on two legs and takes off at high speed.

50 Shades of Green

When it comes to describing the animal world, scientists get ultra specific. So while this reptile is commonly known as the green anole lizard, it's not just green. It's lime green, not parrot green, grass green, or any of the other 48 greens listed in the *Color Catalogue for Field Biologists*. What happens when the green anole changes colors to reflect its mood, temperature, and health? Back to the book!

Like geckos, **green anole lizards** have **sticky** foot pads for **crawling** up trees and walls.

Scientific Name: Anolis carolinensis
Size: 5 to 8 inches
Habitat: Southeastern United States
Diet: Small insects and spiders

Who You Looking At?

Green anoles are highly territorial. A sideways glance from another lizard can send them racing to show who's in charge. It doesn't matter if that other lizard is real or not. When zookeepers show anoles their reflection in a mirror, they show that mirror who's boss!

Old Timers

Admired for their slow and steady nature, eastern box turtles are the official reptile of not one but two states. Models of leisure and healthy living, these turtles can live to be more than a hundred years old. And just like people, they get wrinkles in their shells as they age!

Scientific Name:
Terrapene carolina
Size: 4 to 6 inches
Habitat: Near freshwater in the eastern United States
Diet: A wide variety of small plants and animals

If you see a **box turtle** with red eyes, it's probably **male**.

Lock Box

When this turtle wants some privacy, it doesn't just hide inside its domed shell. It pulls down its shell and locks it. But boxers aren't total loners. In winter months, they burrow under the mud to brumate with other turtles.

Walking the Tightrope

First lesson of being an arboreal alligator lizard: Never look down. These tree dwellers move slowly across slender branches swaying in the breeze, high in the mysterious cloud forests of Mexico and Central America. They have the rare ability to sense toxins in insects and spiders without touching them. At the scent of danger, these lizards quickly jump away. A long tail can lend a hand if they fall. But they still might wish there was a net to catch them!

Cold Hearted

Like all reptiles, arboreal alligator lizards are cold blooded. They can't make their own body heat. Instead, they seek out sunlight to stay warm and avoid cold temperatures.

Scientific Name: Abronia graminea
Size: Up to 7 inches
Habitat: Mexico and Central America
Diet: Insects and spiders

Lizards are often found in the **native legends** and myths of **Central** and **South America.**

Golden Eye

The name's Frog. Spotted Tree Frog. Found only on the exotic island of Madagascar, the spotted malagasy tree frog lives undercover, relying on a variety of techniques to elude predators, including a coat of spy-worthy deadly toxins. Face to face with danger, Agent Rain Forest often relies on his good looks to escape. With a high jump, he flashes the red streaks on his legs. The bright color surprises attackers, allowing our hero enough time to hop away.

Scientific Name:
Boophis picturatus
Size: Up to 1.25 inches
Habitat: Rain forests
of Madagascar
Diet: Small insects

Spotted Malagasy **tadpoles** have the **unusual** ability to **digest** sand.

Made You Look

Frogs develop different styles of jumping depending on where they live. Frogs that burrow underground stay low when they hop. Tree frogs are on the other end of the spectrum, using short, steep jumps to get around.

Here Be Dragons

Komodo dragons have a long, forked tongue. Alligators have bony skin, perfect for warding off medieval swords. And long ago, pterosaurs had big, strong leathery wings. Scientists haven't found an animal that can breathe fire, but some beetles can spray chemicals that burn human skin. And eels are famous for their electric tails. Cast a spell bringing all those elements together, and you just might have the makings of a dragon!

A Low Blow

Komodos are fierce hunters. How can such a squat animal take down something the size of a deer? First it lunges for the feet and knocks it off balance. Then it pounces for the neck. The komodo has sharp, serrated teeth, perfect for ripping into a fresh catch. Its mouth also holds a deadly venom that will kill prey within a week if the attack is interrupted. When a dragon does eat, it will feast on everything from the bones to the hide.

Scientific Name:
  Varanus komodoensis
Size: Up to 10 feet
Habitat: Islands in Indonesia
Diet: Deer, boar, goat, and
  other animals

Want to talk badly about a **komodo?** Use a high-pitch **scream** or a **low voice** to say something outside of the lizard's range of hearing.

Defying Gravity

Like a totem pole, the caledonian crested gecko welcomes you to a strange planet ruled by reptiles. Here, the hairier your feet, the higher you'll climb. Geckos are famous for climbing on smooth trees, walls, and even upside down on the ceiling. Each foot is covered with thousands of tiny hairs called "setae." The hairs form atomic bonds with the surface of whatever they're climbing on. Scientists are studying their feet to design robots, space suits, and climbing gloves for humans.

Crested geckos lick their **eyeballs** to keep them **wet.**

Scientific Name: Correlophus ciliatus
Size: Up to 10 inches
Habitat: Islands between Fiji and Australia
Diet: Insects and plants

Gecko Echo

Geckos chirp, click, squeak, cackle, and bark at each other. The sounds help them attract mates and frighten predators.

Not a Mellow Yellow

In the animal world, bright colors often mean, "Don't you dare." Many poisonous animals use their colors to warn predators to stay away. The fire salamander's back oozes chemicals that poison animals that try to eat it. But the fire salamander doesn't wait for predators to bite. If one gets too close, it sprays those same chemicals at its enemy!

Scientific Name:
  Salamandra salamandra
Size: 6 to 12 inches
Habitat: Forests across
  Europe
Diet: Insects and worms

Most **amphibians** hatch from eggs, but the fire **salamander** develops inside its mother's body.

First in Line

The fire salamander isn't any more salamander-like than any other salamander. But it was the first salamander to be scientifically named, so it gets to be known as *Salamandra salamandra.*

Viper Versus Everyone

Every night, the great lakes bush viper lies waiting to ambush its prey. It relies on its heightened sense of smell, sharp eyesight, and sensitive scales to capture its food. When a rodent, bird, or reptile scurries by, it strikes with vicious speed. With a single bite, fangs release deadly venom, and the battle ends the way it always does. Whatever prey dares to rumble with the viper, this snake always wins.

Best Fang Forward

Vipers, cobras, and rattlesnakes have fangs in the front of their mouths, which make it easy to snag fast-moving prey. Other snakes have fangs in the back for slower, more leisurely bites. But wherever the fangs are, humans do best to avoid them!

Scientific Name: Atheris nitschei
Size: 15 to 30 inches
Habitat: Lakes and wetlands across Africa
Diet: Rodents, small birds, and reptiles

Ophidiophobia is the (totally reasonable) **fear** of **snakes**.

Impressive Patterns

Many reptiles are covered in scales, the small plates of skin that hold in moisture and act as armor against predators. Unlike fish scales, reptile scales are all connected in a single sheet. Crocodiles, turtles, and some lizards have bony scales. Other scales are more flexible. Snake scales are positioned to keep snakes slithering forward, not side to side or backward. Their colors and patterns warn other animals which scales hide venom that can kill.

Primal Predator

Dragons in the Sky

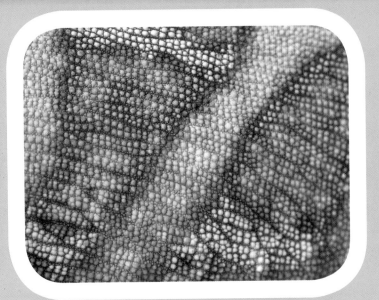

Good Karma Chameleon

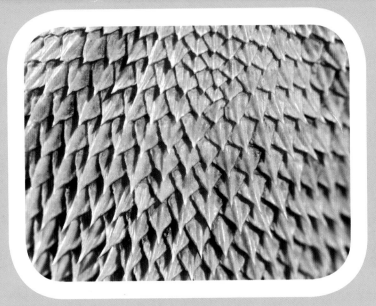

Beard Envy

Tic-Tac Crocodile

Shiver Me Timbers Snake

Poised to Poison

Poison dart frogs are some of the deadliest animals in the world. Their toxins pack a punch potent enough to kill 10 people. While most frogs are nocturnal, these frogs are active in the day, so no one can miss their bright colors or their message: Bite me, and you'll regret it!

(WWF)
Wrestling with Frogs

Male frogs wrestle for territory and mates. Females throw down when it comes to claiming a nest for their eggs. The first one that flips a frog on its back wins!

Scientific Name: Ranitomeya amazonica
Size: 1 to 2 inches
Habitat: Tropical forests in the Amazon
Diet: Ants, termites, and other small insects

Poison frogs have **toxins** in their **skin**, but frogs raised in **captivity**, away from the plants and insects found in their natural **habitat**, don't appear to be poisonous and can be handled **safely** by experts.

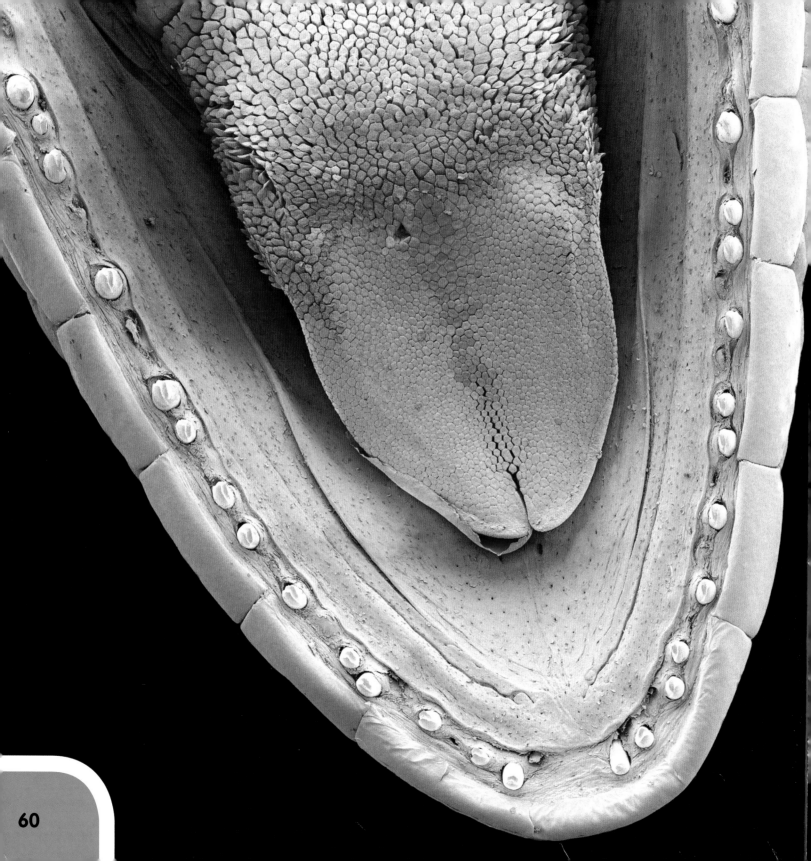

Say "Ahh!"

With a steady diet of crunchy bugs and insects, geckos aren't known for their minty fresh breath, but like all reptiles, they release moisture when they exhale. It's not a lot, but it's enough to dry a gecko out. They may keep their stinky breath to themselves most of the time, but to avoid getting thirsty while they sleep, standoffish geckos cuddle. By staying close, they pool their moisture and help each other wake up refreshed and hydrated.

Ancient Ancestors

Reptiles, birds, and mammals all evolved from amphibians, which were some of the first animals to live on land. Today there are more than 5,000 amphibian species and twice as many reptile species hopping, crawling, climbing, and slithering across the Earth.

Behind the Lens

Now it's your turn! Grab a camera, and start shooting whenever you see something that amazes you or makes you curious to learn more. If you want to go macro without spending too much money, snap a macro lens band over a cellphone camera. Whatever camera you use, these tips will help you get started.

The flash lights the subject.

The shutter acts like a camera, opening and closing to let light into the camera for short periods of time.

The lens is the curved piece of glass that light travels through before reaching a sensor or film inside the camera.

A tripod keeps the camera steady.

The size of the opening in the lens is the aperture. It's measured in fractions.

The focal point is the part of the image that's sharp.

The depth of field is the distance between the parts of an object that are in focus. In micro and macro photography, this distance is very small.

Some lenses have a short focal length and produce a wider angle of view. Other lenses have a longer focal length.

Aperture Scale

| f/1.4 | f/2.8 | f/5.6 | f/8 | f/16 | f/22 |

Large aperture ————————————→ Small aperture
More light strikes image sensor ————————→ Less light strikes image sensor
Shallow Depth of Field (Focus) ————————→ Deep Depth of Field (Focus)

Index